White
Spells
for
Love

About the Author

Originally from Cuba, Ileana Abrev now lives in Queensland, Australia, where she has her own spiritual practice and conducts workshops on magic, spirituality, meditation, chakras, and crystals. She has built a reputation for herself as a respected white witch among her customers and clients. With knowledge passed down to her from her father, an esteemed Santero, Ileana guides customers on a daily basis to solve problems with magic spells and positive visualization. She has been a practicing witch for over ten years.

White Spells for Love

Ileana
Abrev

Llewellyn Publications
Woodbury, Minnesota

First Edition
First Printing, 2008

Book design by Steffani Sawyer
Editing by Brett Fechheimer
Cover design by Lisa Novak
Cover art and interior illustrations by Mary Ross
Llewellyn is a registered trademark of Llewellyn Worldwide, Ltd.

Library of Congress Cataloging-in-Publication Data
Abrev, Ileana, 1959–
    White spells for love / Ileana Abrev.—1st ed.
        p.   cm.
    Includes index.
    ISBN: 978-0-7387-1315-1
    1. Magic. 2. Love—Miscellanea. I. Title.
    BF1623.L6A27 2008
    133.4'42—dc22

                                                2007037807

Llewellyn Worldwide does not participate in, endorse, or have any authority or responsibility concerning private business transactions between our authors and the public.

All mail addressed to the author is forwarded but the publisher cannot, unless specifically instructed by the author, give out an address or phone number.

Any Internet references contained in this work are current at publication time, but the publisher cannot guarantee that a specific location will continue to be maintained. Please refer to the publisher's website for links to authors' websites and other sources.
Note: These spells are not to be used in lieu of professional advice.

Llewellyn Publications
A Division of Llewellyn Worldwide, Ltd.
2143 Wooddale Drive, Dept. 978-0-7387-1315-1
Woodbury, Minnesota 55125-2989, U.S.A.
www.llewellyn.com

Printed in the United States of America

Also by Ileana Abrev

White Spells
White Spells for Protection
Charm Spells

contents

To all my friends who have found love,
and to the ones who still look for it at every turn.
Don't despair; your time is near.

Love and Magic

I asked a few of my friends what love means to them, but apparently that question is more difficult to answer than I thought it would be. I had expected that everyone would know what love means to them, but none of my friends had a spontaneous answer for me, leaving me totally bemused. After my friends had time to give the question some thought, though, I did receive answers:

Love is to trust someone completely and to care about their well-being above your own. Love is devotion and independence, admiration and respect. Love is having someone who brings out the best in you. Love is a connection that makes you smile every time you see the other person. Love is a comfortable feeling of well-being and affection.

Love is a deep desire to protect the one you love. Love is friendship, honesty, happiness, affection, and sharing. Love is contentment, companionship, passion, and desire. Love is finding that missing piece that completes you. Love is friendship, kindness, and the little things that matter. Love is pure happiness. Love is the feeling that you don't want anything to change—ever! Love is when you find yourself mirrored in someone else. Love is everlasting and unconditional. Love is friendship, family, and children. Love is growing old together.

All of this is well and true, but what really *is* love? We keep asking ourselves this question over and over, and the only thing we know about love is that it feels no hate, it has no anger, and it sees no fault. Love is blind to defects and it speaks many languages. It sees no race or color except the color of the soul. Love brings happiness and laughter; it brings joy and enchantment. Love gives people strength, understanding, and courage—but most of all, love forgives and holds no hatred or malice.

When you first feel love, it's like a hidden trigger that activates unknowingly and automatically. "Why am I feeling this way?" you ask yourself when you experience the alien sensations—the weakness in your knees, the butterflies in the pit of your stomach. You aren't able to explain why you can't eat or drink, why you can't concentrate or make sense of your thoughts and feelings; you definitely can't explain your inner hunger to see the other person again. But if you have all of these symptoms, the diagnosis is simple: you're falling in love.

Some people say that love is nothing more than a heightened state of physical attraction, and it's true that being alone and feeling lonely can manifest feelings of love for another. Are you sure you're in love, or are you just lonely for companionship? This is a question you should ask yourself when you think you're in love—because if it's not real love, it won't be everlasting.

An elderly couple walking down the street holding hands is, to me, one of the most beautiful sights there is. If that isn't everlasting love, I don't know what is. Imagine everything that couple has gone through together: the ups and downs of life, the everyday little niggling, their first fight, their first child—not to mention grandchildren and declining health due to age. We all want this type of love; we want the friendship, the companionship, and the "in sickness and in health" bit. The problem is how to find love like that, how to keep it and hold it for the rest of your life.

That's the type of love I and others call romantic love. Romantic love has no gender limitations; it's the love associated with relationships, and it's invigorating, exciting, and emotionally exhausting. Romantic love can sometimes be hurtful, but it laughs because it holds no anger or resentment. The best thing about romantic love is that it can forgive over and over again wholeheartedly no matter how many times the same wrong was done by the one you love.

Romantic love can move mountains when it's appreciated, when it's treated with deep, unconditional affection and respect. It is responsible for the solid and durable happiness in our lives, and without romantic love we may feel we have no purpose. We can spend a lifetime trying to find a soul mate, vowing not to stop trying until we actually do find the romantic, everlasting love we've always wanted.

The older we get, the more we want romantic love, and the more we appreciate its endurance. Those who maintain that they don't want this enduring love are only kidding themselves. Everyone wants someone else in their life; it's part of human nature. We *need* love. We need to receive love and give love, but in order for us to exist in harmony with those around us, love must be given and received unconditionally. If we can accomplish this, the possibility that we'll live a full and meaningful loving life is endless.

I remember watching an old black-and-white movie when I was younger in which one of the male characters said to a woman: "You are beautiful because you are loved."

That line of dialogue has stayed with me throughout my life—and the older I get, the more I appreciate the value of those words. "Beauty is in the eye of the beholder" may be an oft-used phrase, but that doesn't make it any less true. When you are blinded by the beauty within a person and not necessarily by their exterior facade, you love that person unconditionally without scrutinizing their looks, faults, or material circumstances.

People obviously also worry about money, their jobs, and their families, but I can honestly say that at least 75 percent of the people who come to see me for spiritual guidance do so because of issues relating to love—such as how to find it, keep it, and heal it. And they ask me: can I use magic to get it?

Magic is what dreams are made of. Magic is the air we breathe and the memories we cherish. It's an energy itching to manifest our innermost desires. Magic is the power of positive thinking. Magic can't be seen, but it can be felt, and that's what makes it mythical and mystical. Magic is the vessel that carries our wishes to the universe.

Why not project your desires of love to the universe and manifest the love you've always wanted? This can easily be achieved with positive visualization. Everyone consciously visualizes the unreachable and says, "I wish I could have that," projecting their needs and wants with positive visualizations designed to cause intentional changes, a direction of will to accomplish goals and desires. When these goals and desires do manifest, people call it magic, because what they had thought was impossible has now come to be. These manifestations are indeed magic at its best, and by adding items such as herbs, a few candles, or even crystals to your positive visualizations, you create magical spells.

A spell is the reinforcement of a positive visualization. In spells, objects with natural energies are used, such as candles, herbs, or crystals. Each of these objects represents and reinforces the art of positive magic, and they are what I call "the tools." Without these tools, a positive thought sent out to the universe is just a positive visualization.

The tools needed in conjunction with a spell keep you focused on the task at hand. For example, imagine that a dear friend has recently gone through a relationship break-up. You wish her strength to cope with her broken heart, and you decide to turn to magic to aid her pain. As you start to gather the tools needed for the spell, your mind is already focused on one thing—your friend! This focus reinforces your intent, and you begin to build an energy that can't be seen but is certainly felt and heard by the universe.

The universe is out there waiting for our wishes, and I can assure you these wishes do get seen to and are very much scrutinized. Remember that the universe is looking for sincerity in our spells, not just wants based on a whim. Love magic should not be used in any way to manipulate love. It distresses me to know there are people out there who will go to any length to manipulate love and who will stop at nothing to get it.

A few practice something very alarming, something I call *dark love*. I've been asked on numerous occasions to practice dark love on a person someone believes is their everlasting love. Unfortunately, those who come to me for this purpose don't listen to reason. They want results for something I know will only bring sadness—and at times misfortune—to the innocent, and karmic retaliation against those who seek it.

I refuse to have anything to do with such manipulations, and I always remind people of the consequences. But there are those who are so infatuated with a particular individual that they are willing to do anything to obtain their love, a love that is definitely not reciprocated. Turning to dark love is an act that is not tolerated by the laws of the universe or by anyone who is true to their magical workings. The obsessions of those who desire it have blinded their better judgment, as they think they deserve to have someone else against that person's will.

I tell those who seek it that this type of magic will never last—even if the universe decides to grant their desire due to one of many reasons, perhaps simply to provide a learning experience. I want to stress again that dark love never lasts. The bewitchment wears off! When that happens, the manipulator and the individual who conducted the dark-love spell for money must answer to the universe and the Goddess! A lesson should be learned here: don't make a mockery out of love.

I always ask the ones who seek this type of magic, "If this person doesn't love you, why do you want to pursue them?" If I were in that position, I know what I'd do! I'd put on my high heels and look for someone who does love me.

When two people come together, they come together because they were meant to do so. Dark love will never succeed, no matter how much its practitioners try to interfere, because those who try to break the bonds of another's true love will never succeed. If a bond of true love is broken, it will only be broken for a short time; everything always goes back to where it should be—in perfect love and perfect trust for the one for whom the love was meant.

The difference between love magic and *dark*-love magic is very clear, and it's a simple difference to identify. If you are very attracted to a particular person and you feel a connection, but the other person isn't willing to come forward, then that's an example of a time when it's appropriate to practice love magic. Light a pink candle in the name of the person you like. Ask the universe for this person to come forward and tell you their feelings toward you.

If this person comes to you in the next few days and tells you they care for you as much as you care for them, then you'll know it was meant to be; you just hurried along the inevitable. But if the other person tells you they don't want to take it any further, then you must let them go, because that person is not for you.

Now, dark love works differently. If the person you like tells you your feelings are not reciprocated, but you aren't willing to let this person go no matter what the universe says, then you are entering the world of dark love. People practicing dark-love magic may even go so far as to cowardly sneak into the home of another and grab that person's most intimate essences, such as their hairbrushes or even unwashed underwear, in order to take those items to the practitioner of dark love, who will use the essence of the unfortunate love object's soul to manipulate them into submission. The only rationale for this behavior is that the one seeking dark-love magic feels they were denied love—no, not love, but infatuation—from the person on whom they are now preying.

To love someone is to let that person go if they don't want to stay. Nothing is more honorable than to walk away with your head high because you love someone so much that you are willing to let them go so they can find happiness with the person they want to be with. This is love at its best, and it's behavior that should be modeled for those who aren't willing to let go when their hearts are no longer wanted.

Always stay on the right side of karma, working together in unison with the universe. Use love magic in a positive way, to bring only good things to you and your wishes for love.

Anyone can do the fun and easy spells in this book. You can easily tap your love needs and send them to the universe; I can assure you that you will definitely find spells in this book that relate to your present circumstances.

As I've said before, the love spells you choose will be the vessels that carry your love needs to the universe. You have nothing to lose and only love to gain. Who in their right mind doesn't want that?

In the first part of this book, you will learn how to love yourself, the main ingredient in finding and keeping romantic love—there can never be romantic love without self-love. Self-love is the love you have for yourself no matter if you weigh 130 pounds or 330 pounds. It's the love that comes from the pit of your stomach, an unconditional love. Self-love is the acceptance of your decisions and actions, allowing you to attract romantic love. The good news is that a little love magic can help you learn to love yourself!

After you read this book, I predict you will find love and keep it. You will be able to understand love magic and use it to your advantage, always in a positive way. You will be able to do attraction spells, love spells, "honey-do" spells, and more. You will heal love and sexually enhance lovemaking. You will be able to heal a broken heart to accept the breakup of a relationship, and move on to make room for another. You will also learn spells for strengthening relationships, and love spells to keep your relationship interesting where it counts! Moreover, you'll discover how to keep your partner happy—and help you with chores around the house.

Blessed be to all who look for love in the pages of this book. May you find it, keep it, and forever hold it.

Ileana

~ one ~

Getting Started: The "Love Box"

The first step to finding, healing, and keeping love is to gather together some magical tools. Fortunately, you won't need anything that is difficult to find in order to do the spells in this book. On the contrary, your local supermarket and home-and-garden center are among your best magical suppliers—not to mention, of course, magic-oriented websites or any New Age stores that may be in your area. As I've also noted in my other books, items needed for magic do not need to be expensive; they just need to be durable and workable.

Depending on the spells you wish to do, it's good to have some items around the house associated with love. Keep these items in a box, preferably a pink one, and label it fondly as the *Love Box*. In your Love Box, you should keep candle holders, maybe four. You should also add to the box pink candles, any size, but preferably long, tapered ones as they are the best for magical workings.

With any candles you purchase for magical purposes, ensure that the color of the candle will remain consistent once the candle begins to burn. Sometimes a candle may appear pink, or let's say blue, but underneath that color the candle is white. Unfortunately, this inconsistency sends mixed messages to the universe, something you want to avoid when doing a spell since your intent needs to be precise and consistent. So make sure that any candles you buy are truly the color called for in the instructions for each individual spell, both inside and out.

While we're on the subject of candles, you should know that there are also star-sign candle colors. Each individual star sign is associated with a color, and you will be using candles of these colors for some of the spells you'll do. On the next page is a quick guide to star-sign candle colors to get you started.

Aries	March 21–April 19	White
Taurus	April 20–May 20	Red
Gemini	May 21–June 21	Red
Cancer	June 22–July 22	Green
Leo	July 23–August 22	Red
Virgo	August 23–September 22	Black
Libra	September 23–October 22	Black
Scorpio	October 23–November 21	Brown
Sagittarius	November 22–December 21	Gold
Capricorn	December 22 –January 19	Red
Aquarius	January 20–February 18	Blue
Pisces	February 19–March 20	White

Now back to your Love Box.

It is a good idea to put ribbons in the box. They can be ribbons of any color you like, but make sure that pink and red are the dominant colors, since these are the colors associated with love and passion. You can also add lavender and rose essential oils to the box, as well as rose petals, apple seeds, rosemary fresh leaves, lavender leaves, even crystals such as rose quartz or any others you like that you think are related to love and attracting love.

You can even put in your Love Box a statue or image of your favorite love goddess, perhaps the Greek goddess Aphrodite or the Roman goddess Venus. Even before you finish putting together your Love Box, you will already be sending signals of love to the universe. While you put your box together, your thoughts will be on finding or healing love, so in actual fact you will have done your first spell, the Love Box spell. And don't limit your box to the items I've suggested! Concentrate, and let your thoughts and feelings dictate what else you add to your Love Box that is relevant to your love needs.

When you think your Love Box is ready, keep it in a special place and don't share its contents with anyone. This box is something private between you and the universe, and no one else. You don't even have to tell anyone about it. In fact, sometimes it's preferable that you don't. People question things they don't understand, which can create a negative energy around you. And when you conduct magic, you need all the positive energy you can get.

You need to know about other energies with which you will be working. One of them is our beloved moon—the "lady of the night," as I call it. The moon is very important in any type of magical workings, as we can tap into the moon's energy to obtain that which we want. A full moon occurs when the moon is bright, round, and at its greatest potential; this is a time for any type of magical workings, especially love spells. After the full moon is the waning moon, when the moon starts to decrease. This is a good time to work against opposing forces, such as an old partner who still can't accept a breakup and is making your new relationship hard to get off the ground.

Then there's the new moon, which is hidden and cannot be seen. The new moon is also a good time for all types of love spells. Between the new moon and the full moon, the moon is waxing and growing. As it grows, its potential is endless, and this is a great time to work on enhancing your love and relationship needs—because as the moon grows full so does the love you want and need.

The days of the week are just as important as the moon. Each day has a relationship to a planet, a relationship you will use to conduct magic on the appropriate days. Let's start with Sunday. Its relation is the sun, and Sundays are a good time to conduct healing spells for love. Monday is related to the moon, and Monday is a great day of the week to protect love. Tuesday is associated with Mars, and on Tuesdays you should conduct strength and courage love spells. Wednesday is associated with Mercury; on Wednesdays it is best to conduct spells for communication, as the planet Mercury is the problem-solver of the planets. Thursdays, related to Jupiter, are for legal matters on love. Venus is associated with Fridays, and it is best to conduct love rituals on a Friday. Saturday is related to Saturn; on this day you will be doing spells against negative love forces.

Before you start doing the spells in this book, find a place that is quiet so you can have total privacy to be in tune with the universe and your needs. When you say a specified rhyme or chant for a spell, make sure that it is true to your heart. Believe the words you speak in order to convey your sincerity to the universe. The universe is there waiting to hear your needs, as is our beloved Goddess. She will grant your wishes if they are yours to have, but don't ever get discouraged with magic. It takes time, and you need to be patient because if it's meant to be, it will be and, if not, the Goddess has an even better plan for your romantic love.

The keys to spellworking are to stay positive and to really mean what you want. Sincerity, honesty, and wanting what is best for yourself without hurting others along the way are the most important parts of magic. If you do harm others, you will have to answer to the Threefold Law: "Harm none; for if you do, it will pay you back in threes."

two

Love Yourself: Spells for Self-love

It's all fair and good that you want romantic love, the everlasting love about which you have dreamed since you were seven years old. But before you can achieve this type of love, you need to know if you love the most important part of your world—and that most important part is *you*. Yes, you. Because if you don't love yourself, no one else will.

There is a simple test to discover if your sense of self-love is healthy, but don't feel embarrassed in any way when you do this test, and don't laugh! No, don't laugh, as this is very serious stuff. The test is to take off all your clothes and stand totally naked in front of a full-length mirror. See yourself in your birthday suit . . . and start scrutinizing yourself. Let me tell you that you are your worst critic. I know, I've done this exercise. Now, as seriously as you can possibly be, look deep into your own eyes and ask yourself, "Do I love me?"

This is the most difficult question you are ever going to ask yourself, but you need to know whether or not you love yourself unconditionally with all of the faults you *think* you possess. You need to look at the things that bother you about yourself and deal with them. If you can't change them, accept them and let them be a part of your life. Look at every dimple and every wrinkle, every scar and blemish, and accept them into your space and love the person you have become.

If you liked and loved what you saw in front of the mirror as you scrutinized yourself, you will have no difficulties finding the romantic love you've always wanted. But if you truly didn't like what you saw, or if you don't accept yourself for who you really are, then you have a lot of work to do to repair the self-love you lack.

If you feel negative about yourself and the way you look, those around you will also feel the negativity you unknowingly emit; unfortunately, these negative energies have the ability to break or make a romantic love. These energies are like minute beams of light that, when distorted by a negative thought, feel like small electric shocks to others' etheric fields, acting as a repellent.

The etheric field is a projection of pure energy that is all around us. Being within it is similar to being inside a large bubble of light bouncing with vibrating positive energies— but only when it's healthy, only when you feel good about who you are and when you love the person you see in the mirror every day. If you have doubts about self-love or if you have low self-esteem, the etheric field around you will break, and emit those minute electrical charges that repel others.

We are attracted to one another in both physical and ethereal ways. When you first meet someone, that person is of course attracted by your looks—but only for a split second. Physical attraction concerns what we as individuals find attractive, but that attraction can disappear quickly depending on ethereal attraction, or the attraction of the energies we emit. No matter how physically attractive you find someone, if their ethereal energies are filled with doubt, low self-esteem, anger, remorse, or a lack of self-love, then attraction alone is not going to create romantic, everlasting love—because ethereal attraction will always trump physical attraction.

In essence, the people around you feel the insecurities you have. They feel your troubled mind, if it is troubled, and only because they've felt a trickle of your lack of confidence. You can't afford these electrical leaks when they are visible to others' ethereal fields, but the good news is that these types of leaks can be avoided if you start to think positively about yourself and the way you live your life.

Three ways of repairing and enhancing self-love

1. Affirmations
Affirmations help to seal the ethereal field from emitting negative and doubtful energies. By doing affirmations, you are affirming yourself, the way you feel about who you are,

and the imperfections you think you possess. An affirmation sends your message to the universe, and the universe listens and responds with positive manifestations.

When you do an affirmation, you must believe in what you are affirming. Make sure your affirmations are sincere and from the heart, and that you believe in what you are saying without fear. You are worthy to affirm your wishes, because you want to love and trust yourself and accept who you are.

An affirmation works in the same way as positive visualization. By speaking aloud an affirmation, you trigger your subconscious mind into thinking and feeling positively about yourself. More often than not, people tend to speak and think more negative words and ideas than they do positive ones. Affirming a positive thought enables us to achieve what we want. An affirmation may work straightaway or it may take some time to process through the subconscious mind; it depends on how long you've been thinking negatively about yourself.

Affirmations should be said first thing in the morning, when your mind is at its freshest and not yet polluted with negative thoughts, and they should also be said at any time you wish during the day. Repeat an affirmation right after you think negatively about yourself. Remember that the more you say your affirmations, the more chances you'll have to start thinking positively about yourself. Think of your mind as a computer; you're installing an "I love myself" program and uninstalling an "I don't like myself" program. Always remember to affirm in the present tense. You want to love yourself *now* and for always, not just in the future, because you want romantic love and you want it now.

Affirmation for self-love and acceptance:
I love me because I am me.
Inner beauty resides within me.
I'm the light of love that radiates warmth and self-acceptance.
And the person I'm most comfortable with is me.

2. The self-love pouch spell

Now that you have your affirmation, you are going to put together a pouch that you can carry with you or hang around your neck. It doesn't matter what material you use for the pouch as long as the color is pink.

In addition to the pink pouch, you will need:

- 1 rose quartz
- 1 small piece of blue paper (write on it "I love _____[your name]")
- Wooden shavings from a sharpened pencil (no lead)
- 1 cooking clove
- 2–3 drops of rose essential oil
- 1 small twig full of rosemary leaves

Once you have gathered all of the above, place each item separately into the pouch. As you put each item in the pouch, visualize self-love and loving yourself for who you are. This may be a good time for you to say your affirmation over and over again. By doing so, you will be sending to the universe your thoughts of love for yourself, and at the same time you will be energizing your pouch. Once you have finished your pouch, wear it or have it with you at all times and at night place it under your pillow.

3. Rid of the old self bath spell

A bath is a good way to utilize the water element to its fullest potential. Water is our emotions, the emotions that run through our veins and through our everyday thoughts. These are the emotions we carry deep within us, emotions we keep hidden from the rest of the world. To obtain self-love, you are going to wash out those old thought patterns because there isn't any room for them when you want romantic love.

You will need:
- 1 black candle
- 1 white candle
- 1 teaspoon of olive oil
- 2 drops of rose oil
- 1 tablespoon of wheat germ oil
- ½ cup of rock salt

Rub the olive oil on the black candle and visualize all that you wish to let go about yourself that you don't like. Then rub the rose oil on the white candle while visualizing the love you want for yourself.

Now light both candles and place them inside the bathroom. Draw a warm bath, and add the rock salt with the wheat germ oil to the bathwater. Once you are in the bath, submerge yourself and think of all you wish to let go about yourself. Wet your hair, relax underwater, and let your fears penetrate the water. (But make sure the salty water doesn't get into your eyes or mouth.)

Once you've finished, don't rinse. Pat yourself dry instead. Look at the water, and in the water see all that you have just let go of and never wish back. Pull the plug and wave goodbye to your old ways and smile because you are now a different person, a person who loves who they are. Don't wash your hair or your body for a full twenty-four hours, as you want to stop that which you have just let go of from ever coming back.

three

The Breakup:
Spells to Mend a Broken Heart

The breakup of a relationship can be detrimental to your emotional state of mind, and can take you into what I and others call "the abyss." The abyss is a dark, lonely place, uncertain and unfamiliar, filled with your own negative thoughts. After the breakup of a romantic relationship, the emotional pain and exhaustion can leave you totally devastated to the point of no return. Your desire to move on often does not exist. You can't concentrate, your heart no longer beats with life, and the word *love* suddenly takes on a totally different meaning.

Believe it or not, you have created this abyss as a safety zone. Feeling safe within your abyss means that you don't have to face the world and its responsibilities. But the longer you stay in the abyss, the deeper you go into its darkness until you aren't able to focus on anything but your own disappointment.

We've all been there, and I know it's definitely not a pleasant experience. You'll know you've reached the depths of the abyss when physical illness, generated by self-absorption, engulfs your defenses.

The universe knows we all react differently to any specific emotional pain or hurt, but the universe also allows us a grieving period. Embrace this time and use this period to learn and evolve into another stage of spiritual growth. But when you hear a voice telling you it's time to move on, you'll know the mourning hour has now passed and it is time to embrace rebirth.

Baby steps

After a romantic breakup, the first thing you need to do is lift your self-esteem because you will not be feeling good about the way you look. Go to the person who styles your hair to ask them about getting a new look, or get a gym membership and start toning your body.

Go through your bedroom and closets, and put anything that belonged to your ex into a box. Leave it in your garage or another out-of-the-way place, and ask your ex to take the box away as soon as possible. Then go through your own things and give away to charity everything you no longer want. You can throw away or burn the items that remind you of memories you'd rather forget, like those old sexy nightgowns you'll need to retire for new ones. Those memories of your relationship are no longer a part of your soon-to-be world.

The next big step is to rid yourself of all of your bedding. Pillows, sheets, blankets—all of it! You've shared your most intimate times in that bed, and it's time to get rid of all that was. If you're financially able to do so, buy a new mattress; if you're not, sprinkle cleaning ammonia, salt, and dry rosemary leaves on the mattress to rid it of all the energies you don't wish to remember. Let that mixture sit on the mattress for about an hour, and then vacuum away the past. Replace the bedding with fresh coverings, preferably in happy and warm colors to keep you cozy. If you do all this, I can assure you that the bed bugs of your old relationship will never bite back.

Spells for your emotional well-being

Strength of steel

Moping for a lost love can make you feel weak and lifeless, since you're constantly thinking about the past without making room for the future. This spell will help you find the inner strength you possess, keeping you strong and focused as each day passes.

You will need:

- 1 red candle
- 1 small hollow tube made of steel, with just one hole on the top
- 1 teaspoon of cumin seeds
- 1 teaspoon of poppy seeds
- 1 small piece of parchment paper
- ½ meter (just over 1½ feet) of red electrical tape

Light the red candle on a Tuesday. Then visualize the candle's flame as the strength you'll need to carry you through the day from the time you wake up.

Write your full name on the parchment paper. Then mix together the poppy seeds and the cumin seeds, placing all of them inside the steel tube. As you do so, say:

> *"My physical and mental being*
> *will be as strong as steel from now on."*

With the red electrical tape, close the top end of the steel tube so that nothing inside it can come out. As you tape up the tube, say:

> *"My strength comes from the inside and*
> *the abyss is no longer a part of my life."*

Keep this tube with you at all times—even under your pillow when you're asleep. In a matter of weeks, you'll start to feel stronger; as the days pass, you will feel your strength increase from within.

When you feel you no longer need the steel tube, remove the electrical tape and scatter the seeds to the wind.

Letting go

Letting go of the past is the key to imagining the future. What's done is done, and the past is exactly that: the *past*. Once you're able to let go of the past, your feelings and attitudes toward your current situation will change, and you'll be able to confront the sadness you feel. Once you've done that, the pain will lessen, new opportunities will find their way to you, and for the first time since the breakup, your soul can be at peace.

You will need:

- 1 black candle
- 2 blue candles
- 1 frankincense incense stick
- 1 white rose
- A bunch of maple or eucalyptus leaves

Take all of the above ingredients to your backyard or to a park on a moonless Saturday night.

Make a circle with the leaves. When you're done, stand in the middle of the circle. Next, light the frankincense incense stick, placing it in the ground just in front of you. Stare at the night sky and visualize that which you wish to let go that is deeply embedded in your heart.

Now, pick up the black candle and embed your fingernails into it. As you do so, visualize all that you wish to let go. Penetrate the candle with your fingernails, which are acting as your magical pen. Then light the candle, place it outside the circle, and say,

> *"Candle flame now you hold that which*
> *I wish to let go and wish no more."*

Light both of the blue candles and place them inside the circle at each side of the incense stick. While you're doing this, visualize the peace you wish to have and the tranquility that comes from letting go of the things you no longer need.

Now pick up the white rose and gently pass it over your entire body in a caressing manner. See it healing, cleansing, and sealing your soul from ever bringing back that which you've just let go.

Sit outside, still in the middle of your now-sacred circle, for as long as you wish. Outside the circle you've made, watch the black candle burn away the past as you feel new-found peace penetrate your heart chakra (your chest).

Let the black candle burn to its end outside, snuff the blue candles, and pick up all the leaves and scatter them into the wind. Wish yourself a good night, and feel satisfied that the past is behind you and new horizons are ahead.

Calming the anger within

Don't blame yourself or the world for what you believe to be your misfortune. First of all, keep in mind that what you're going through is *not* a misfortune. You could blame the entire world for the pain you feel, but doing so will get you nowhere. Instead, think of the experience as another step in your spiritual growth as you move toward a better understanding of love.

You will need:

- A living pine tree
- 2 meters (about 6½ feet) of thick rope
- Pure essential lavender oil

Place four drops of the lavender oil on your hands and quickly rub them together. Next, rub your hands along the length of the rope from top to bottom to distribute the lavender evenly. As you rub in the lavender, visualize the anger you wish to stop and control.

Now, wrap the rope around the pine tree you've found, while saying:

"Pine that keeps the peace within each one of us,
help me to control the anger I now hold.
Don't let me lash out at the ones I love the most
or anyone else."

Tie a knot around the pine tree with the rope. As you do so, visualize the issue or issues that are making you angry. If there is more than one issue making you angry, tie a knot for each one. As you tie each knot, get angry; this is the time you can let it all go! Once you release your anger, you'll leave it in the care of the pine tree and the rope to control.

Forgive and move on

When you're alone after a breakup, your mind acts like a video on automatic rewind, playing back your relationship and pausing at the scenes you wish you could change.

You must forget the "what-ifs" and concentrate on the "what now." Do this by forgiving the person who matters the most—you! Tell yourself the truth: that you did the best you could do at the time.

You will need:

- As many grape seeds as years the relationship lasted (to get the grape seeds, eat the grapes yourself)
- As many corn kernels as years the relationship lasted
- 1 large cinnamon stick
- 1 rose quartz crystal
- 1 pink drawstring bag

Eat the grapes and leave the seeds together outside in a shady place for one day to dry. When you're ready to start the spell, place the cinnamon stick inside the pink draw-string bag and say:

"Love is who I am."

Now add the corn kernels to the drawstring bag and say:

"I forgive myself for years of self-blame."

Add the grape seeds and say:

"The past shall be erased but not forgotten, and replaced by a future bright and full of love."

Finally, place the rose quartz crystal inside the drawstring bag as you say:

"I replace self-blame with self-love, and this is how it's going to be from now on."

Keep the drawstring bag with you at all times; when you think of the past, touch the bag and your thoughts will be focused on the present. The past will never haunt you.

Forgive the ex

I know you're not going to like this, but you also need to forgive your ex-partner in order to move on. The good news is that you don't have to do so in person. To forgive another when they have done you wrong may seem unthinkable, but you can do it if you step over and push aside your ego. Such forgiveness is a sign of maturity and spiritual understanding. You should also keep in mind that holding grudges often darkens your best judgment and inhibits the healing processes.

You will need:

- 1 white candle
- 1 white flower of any kind
- 1 piece of parchment paper
- 1 blue ink pen

Light the white candle on a Wednesday, and on the parchment paper write the following:

I'm a gentle soul who looks for happiness at every turn.
For actions past I need to forgive what another has done.
No longer will I carry the weight of the past on my shoulders,
because I understand that there are imperfections in all of us.
The quicker I forgive, the quicker I can move on and start my new life.

I forgive you, [name], *for _____.*

List all the things you need to forgive, and then write:

So be it.

Sign the paper.

Once you've done all that, wrap the white flower inside the parchment paper. Place the paper outside on the grass during a new moon and keep it outside for one entire night.

On the following day, burn the paper and the flower, and take the ashes to the sea. Throw the ashes as far into the water as possible. If you don't live near an ocean, take the ashes to a running stream.

Emotional health pouch

When you are emotionally vulnerable, your health is at risk. The associated pressures from a broken relationship can put your body under enormous amounts of stress. When this occurs, your body will be a magnet for all types of illness—which, unfortunately, you yourself will have emotionally induced.

You will need:

- 1 teaspoon of sassafras
- 1 garlic clove
- 1 teaspoon of dry angelica
- 1 teaspoon of nutmeg
- 1 walnut
- 3 drops of eucalyptus oil
- ¼ meter (just less than a foot) of white cotton material
- ½ meter (just over 1½ feet) of white silk ribbon

Mix the sassafras, garlic clove, angelica, nutmeg, and walnut together, and then add in the three drops of eucalyptus oil. As you mix together all of these ingredients, say:

"I can't afford to be sick, and sick I will not be from emotions I carry deep within."

Follow this by spreading out the white cotton material, placing all that you have mixed together on top of the material as you say:

"Protected I will be from the invasion of sickness while dealing with emotions I'm working to control within me."

Gather together into a bundle the cotton material with the above items inside it. To keep the bundle closed, tie up the top of it with the white ribbon. Keep the bundle under your pillow for protection against any illnesses.

Spiritually cleansing your home

Whether or not your breakup was amicable, your home needs a good spiritual cleansing from your ex's energies, which no longer belong there. This cleansing is not hard to do, and it's just another step in the process of moving forward. For the best results, wait and do the cleansing once all of your ex's belongings are out of your home and you're alone.

You will need:

- 1 cup of rock salt
- ¼ cup of dry rosemary leaves
- 1 old white cotton cloth
- 1 cup of ammonia (Do not breath it in!)
- ¼ teaspoon of valerian dry herb on a charcoal tablet (Note: valerian can be hard on the nose)

This spell is best done on a Saturday, when you have some time up your sleeve. Burn the valerian on a charcoal tablet and bring this purifying smoke all over your home—even taking it inside your closets and cupboards. As you do so, say over and over again in a loud and happy voice:

> *"New happiness awaits my home
> with no negative actions or thoughts."*

Mix together the rosemary leaves and rock salt, and then go all over your residence once more and sprinkle this mixture over every corner of the floor or carpet, saying over and over again in a loud and happy voice:

> *"Strength, faith, and hope
> I give my home and all who live in it."*

Moisten the white cotton cloth with the ammonia, and then start from the back of your home and, using the cloth, remove your ex's fingerprints from the windows, doorknobs, or any other place where his or her fingerprints could still be.

As you wipe every place where your ex's fingerprints might have been, say over and over again:

> *"To* [name of ex]:
> *I bid you goodbye and farewell.*
> *Your energies are now gone from my place."*

In a matter of minutes, you will experience a newfound feeling of weightlessness and happiness. Your home will once again be a comfort zone for all.

Sadness be gone

Let's concentrate on your future happiness. Don't think for a minute that you're going to stay sad for the rest of your life! You're going through a grieving period, and the universe, aware of your pain, is allowing you time to reflect, grieve, and move on.

You will need

- 2 oranges (cut into six parts)
- 1 lemon (cut into four parts)
- 1 grapefruit (cut into six parts)
- 1 teaspoon of lemongrass

- 4 drops of marjoram essential oil
- 1 yellow candle
- 1 pink candle

Fill the bath with warm water. Then, as you light the candles, visualize the sadness vanishing from your heart. Now add to the bath the oranges, the lemon, and the grapefruit, and watch all of it float to the top. Finally, add the lemongrass and marjoram essential oil.

Mix all these ingredients together in the water, turn off the lights, and get into the bath. While visualizing this bath making your sadness a thing of the past, submerge your head under the water and stay there in total silence for as long as you can hold your breath. Once you surface, all your sadness will be gone and a new happier you will appear in a day or so.

When you've finished with your bath, take the plug out of the bathtub and watch your sadness go down the drain. Collect all the pieces of citrus and place them in the garbage, along with your sadness.

~ four ~

Spells to Go

The one simple thing you need to know about love is that it's all around us. Why not try to bring some of that love into your world? You can do so through simple means, which I call "spells to go." These types of mini-spells are simple and easy to do. In this chapter, you'll use natural energies, such as colors, herbs, and even crystals. These energies will bring forth the spirit of love, which will aid you in attracting others into your space.

For Attraction

Attractive to others I will be
Insert a teaspoon of catnip into a small, red drawstring bag and carry it with you at all times. At night, place it under your pillow.

Sexy—nothing more, nothing less
Stitch to the back of all your undergarments a small red bow to attract those who see past your clothes.

Sweet let me be
Wear perfumes that are sweet, such as rose, lavender, or vanilla-based perfumes.

Cinnamish
Carry a stick of cinnamon with you at all times, and chew a little piece when you want to attract the one you like.

Friday and Monday attraction bath
Have a bath with a teaspoon of honey and five drops of rose oil every Friday and every Monday.

A peach will do

While eating a sweet peach, visualize the love you need. Wash the peach pit in a rose-based cologne and place it outside on the grass on a full moon to draw down the energies from the lady of the night. Afterward, carry the pit with you at all times to attract love into your life.

Elm the tree

Wrap your arms around an elm tree and tell it your deepest love wish. When you are ready to leave, pick from the ground any dead leaves; elm trees like their spaces tidy and clean.

Crystal power

Carry or wear a rose quartz crystal to attract the love within.

Venus comes out to play

Wear pink in the afternoon and preferably red on Friday night, when Venus comes out to play.

Look at me, look at me
Carry a stick of patchouli to attract onlookers.

Hide and seek
Wash your hair with rosemary and you will be noticed by the one you seek to be with.

Relax with chamomile
Dip your index finger in a sweet cup of freshly made chamomile tea. As if it were perfume, anoint the pleasure points on your body with the sweet brew to bring yourself luck in attracting those you desire.

Beautiful
Every morning look at yourself in the mirror and say over and over again as many times as you can in rhyme:

> *"I am beautiful and attractive to me.*
> *I will be thus to all who look and see."*

Yo te adoro
Carry a periwinkle flower to be attractive and adorable to others.

Dreams of love

Burn sandalwood at night and you will have prophetic love dreams of the man or woman you wish to meet.

Lets us share

On a full-moon night, share and eat chestnuts with the one you like. Together the night shall pass and love will come around.

Attraction powder

In a shady place, dry the skin of a pear you have just eaten. Once the skin is crispy and dry, crush it with a mortar and pestle along with a small teaspoon of damiana until it becomes a powder. Before you go out on the town, dust your hands with this power and you will be attractive to those who make eye contact and hand contact with you.

Love wish

Make a love wish with a handful of sunflower seeds and scatter them in the sea or a running stream.

Star bright
Keep a star anise seed with you at all times to bring you the luck you need to find the love of your life.

Little red female bag
To attract women, carry with you patchouli and bay leaves in a little red drawstring bag.

Little red male bag
To attract a man, carry with you a piece of fresh ginger and a few tonka beans in a little red drawstring bag.

Spells to find your romantic love

The first thing you need to do is to start thinking positively about who you want in your life. Remember that wishes do come true—so when you ask for that special someone in your life, make sure you know what you want. Looks do matter, of course, but personality always outshines looks. Have a clear picture of this person; maybe he or she is someone you already know or someone you've always visualized spending the rest of your life with.

Keep this person in your mind's eye both day and night. By doing so, you are letting the universe know that you are now ready to have what you've always wanted—someone in your life to have and to hold. Visualize this person with you 24/7. Think of what it would be like to be with that person all the time, and keep in mind the things you've always wanted to do with the one you love.

Finding your romantic love is similar to getting ready for an exam. In school, you study and study until you know all the answers by heart; that's also what you'll be doing to find your romantic love. You should think, breathe, and visualize this love until you know the other person as well as you know yourself. As you're doing these visualizations, you're telling the universe that you're ready for romantic love. You want your visualizations to be heard and blessed into a wish for love. No matter which spells you do, visualization is the key in any spell to open the doors to the mystical part of the universe, the mystical part that grants wishes of love.

Finding your soul connection

Once during every lifetime we meet a very special person, and with that person we feel and make an indescribably strong connection. You can't possibly imagine your life without this other person. This connection is the recognition of souls who have shared numerous lifetimes and have learned and grown spiritually together. With this spell you will find and keep this soul connection.

You will need:
- 1 bag of pink cotton balls
- 1 white candle
- 1 decanter full of fresh water
- 1 bowl of soil

On a Wednesday night when the full moon is out, go out into your backyard or to a park. Make sure there's no wind. Then make a large semicircle around you with the pink cotton balls, and as you do so keep in your mind visions of the person who you know is your soul mate. After you have done all this, stay in the center of the love circle you've just created.

In the middle of the circle and at your feet, dig a hole small enough to keep your candle upright and balanced. Then light it and say:

"Light of day, light of night,
search for my soul mate in the flames
of this candle this night."

Then let the decanter of water spill on the ground four times, and each time say:

"Across the seas find the one who is also looking for me."

Now grab a handful of the dirt, letting it spill on the ground four times. Say each time:

"Across land, deserts, and mountains, find my soul mate."

Once you've finished, sit on the ground with the candle burning just in front of you. Close your eyes and visualize yourself as a bird flying over mountains, water, and land looking for your soul mate, who will soon come to light.

Before a night on the town

If you're single and out having a good time, you can't help but wonder if you're going to meet someone who is worth bringing home to your mother. With this spell, you'll be able to attract and pick the person you'll want to be with for a long time.

You will need:
- 1 red candle
- 1 white rose
- 1 red rose
- 5 drops of lavender oil
- 3 drops of patchouli oil

Draw a warm bath, turn down the lights, and light the red candle. As you light the red candle, think of the fun you'll be having out on the town. Hold both flowers in your hands and let each petal fall gently on your bathwater. Visualize each petal as someone wanting to meet you and wanting to get to know you.

Now, with each drop of oil that you put in your bathwater, say:

> *"To all I meet, come and talk to me
> because that is the only way you are
> going to get to know and like me."*

Gently step into your now-ready bath and breathe the aromatic essence of love that is penetrating deep into your soul. Relax, because you may be out all night. After your bath, pat yourself dry to seal the energy of attraction you have just created.

One day a bride I will be

Most every little girl has a dream, and that same dream follows her through adulthood: to get married and live happily ever after. There isn't any reason to believe your childhood dreams can't come true; they *can* come true with this doll spell.

You will need:

- 1 doll, with the same hair and skin coloring as you. This doll must be able to sit down and stand up.

- Enough white material to make the doll a wedding dress
- Tulle to make a veil
- Needle, white cotton, and a pair of scissors
- 1 rose quartz crystal

You are going to make a wedding dress for the doll, whom you will call by your own first name. First, design the dress; you can use any material you like as long as it's white. As you design your doll's dress, have in mind the dress *you* will wear on your wedding day.

Tell yourself that the doll is you, and it is you who is getting ready for your wedding day. Make sure not to use a sewing machine, as you must stitch every stitch yourself. It doesn't matter how long it takes you to create your doll bride. You should not be in a rush as you dream of your wedding day and wedding night.

Make the dress first, then the veil. Adorn the doll's hair as you would like your own hair to look at your wedding. Finally, place a rose quartz crystal between the doll's breasts. Sit your doll bride on your bed or stand her up facing the front door of your bedroom. This spell symbolizes you in the future, walking out of your own room all dressed in white on your wedding day.

Pick up the phone and call me

By now, you may have already found someone you want to spend time with. But that love interest may not be calling you as often as you'd like to make a date so romantic love can occur.

You will need:

- Pink ribbon
- 1 rose quartz crystal
- 1 tiger-eye crystal
- 1 glass of water (if you live near an ocean, use sea water)
- 1 teaspoon of rock salt
- 1 small piece of paper

Add the rock salt to the glass of water and submerge both of the crystals in this water. Take the glass out to your backyard and leave it out there for three days and three nights under the stars.

Once you've done this, take the crystals out of the water and rub your hands together until they feel hot and tingly. Then take both crystals into your hands and hold them there, thinking intently of the person you wish would call you. Say out loud:

> *"Remember to call me you will, and other things*
> *I wish you to do to get to know me."*

Write the person's name on the piece of paper, and then wrap the crystals together with the paper and use the ribbon to keep it all in place. Once you've done this, take your little crystal bundle out on a full-moon night and leave it out overnight on the grass. Next, place the bundle by the phone to receive your very important call.

~ five ~

Relationship Spells

In nearly any relationship, romantic love begins to stagnate at a certain point in time. A busy work schedule can override one's personal life, leaving little time for oneself much less someone else; such a schedule is often a major reason for relationship stagnation. Long-established relationships can suffer not because the partners don't love each other, but because they both begin to take each other for granted. Then there are the unique issues of the young relationship, in which people, such as newlyweds, sometimes try too hard to accommodate each other.

In every relationship, there is always something each partner wants to change or make better; this is normal and, at times, justifiable. We wouldn't be human if we didn't seek change and improvement. If your partner isn't accommodating your needs, your first instinct will probably be to "change" them, but sadly such an effort comes across like nagging. I can assure you that nagging will only jeopardize your relationship. Think about it: the only reason someone in a relationship wants this type of change is to accommodate their own needs, not their partner's.

When you first fall in love, you fall in love with everything the other person brings to the relationship, the entire package. If your partner was a slob before you came along, then there is little you can do to force a change in that behavior if your partner doesn't want to change. Yet when you fully accept your partner for who he or she is, then you'll notice that some changes do happen, and as amazing as it may seem, your partner will start to accommodate your needs.

Communication is a big part of all relationships. Sitting down and talking about what's upsetting you is the key to a healthy everlasting relationship, but there's also no reason why you can't use magic to help yourself through the trying times in relationships and to help resolve the minor arguments all couples have.

I need a little help

The last thing you want to do when you get home is housework, but sometimes your partner forgets that the breakfast dishes are still in the sink. This lack of cooperation can cause tension and can make each of you resent the other.

You will need:
- 1 teaspoon of myrtle
- 1 white candle
- 1 red candle
- Half a teaspoon of lemon rind
- A pair of your partner's stinky socks

On a night between the waxing moon and the full moon, set up a small altar with all of the above items when your partner is away from home. Light the white candle and the red candle together while visualizing what you want your partner to do that will make your life just that little bit easier. As you're visualizing, say:

"Help me you will without me saying 'please.'"

Mix the myrtle and the lemon rind together. Once you've done this, divide the mixture into two equal parts and gently stuff each of the socks with the resulting halves of the mixture. As you do so, visualize your partner coming home from work and finishing chores without a fuss.

Take the pair of socks and hide them under your partner's side of the bed. Let the candles consume all the way through, and before you know it, your partner will accomplish the little chores and tasks you've always wanted him or her to do.

Libido come and wake me!

There's always room for more love in the bedroom. Yet sometimes you're too busy even to think about the pleasures that used to bring you and your partner together. A lack of time is often a factor; by the time you go to bed, you may be so tired that falling asleep is the only thing on your mind. You give you partner a loving kiss on the cheek and say goodnight, leaving your partner, who wanted more than just a peck on the cheek, feeling annoyed.

You will need:

- 2 red candles
- A bunch of holly
- ½ cup of sesame seeds
- 1 teaspoon of honey
- 4 drops of rose oil
- 1 red bowl

Draw a warm bath on a full-moon night just before you go to bed with your partner. Light the red candles in your bathroom and visualize the sexual feelings you wish to have so you're not too tired when it's time to play.

Drop the holly in the bathtub and watch it float on top of the bathwater as you visualize yourself swimming in a sea of passion and lust.

In the red bowl, mix together the sesame, the rose oil, and the honey until a paste is made.

Take your clothes off and rub this mixture all over your body, feeling the aroma and the pleasure it brings you. Now turn the lights down, get into your bath, and relax for a little while.

When you're ready to get out of the bathtub, pat yourself dry. Now, while the candles burn with your desires, slip into bed and be ready for the goddess within you to come out and play. Let the candles do their magic by burning all the way down. Do this spell whenever you feel you need to be a goddess again.

Flaming passions

Perhaps you and your partner have been together for so long that passion has become a memory, and it no longer fills up your world. At times you may even think your partner isn't interested in you anymore. Don't worry! This lessening of passion occurs in most long-term relationships; you could even call it a "rite of passage." Such a reduction in passion is destined to occur, but passion can also be reawakened to stir in both of you the feelings you once had for each other, so that you can experience again what once was.

You will need:

- 1 red candle
- ½ teaspoon of vanilla essence
- 2 drops of lilac pure essential oil
- 1 teaspoon of witch's grass
- 1 passion fruit
- 1 teaspoon of honey
- 1 teaspoon of poppy seeds
- 1 small white bowl
- ½ meter (just over 1½ feet) of red ribbon

A week before you do the spell, purchase the large passion fruit and cut it in half. Take out the inner fruit until you are left with only the skin. Place the two halves of the fruit where the skin can dry without sunlight.

On the night you wish to do the spell, place the drops of the lilac oil in the palm your left hand. Then hold the red candle with your right hand. Anoint the candle with the lilac oil by rubbing the candle sensually from the middle of the candle up, then back to the middle of the candle and down, in a slow and deliberate motion. As you do this, remember the passion you and your partner once had. Then, when you're finished and ready to proceed, light the candle.

Combine in the bowl the vanilla essence, honey, poppy seeds, and witch's grass. Mix together well all of these ingredients until a paste is made. (You may need to add in more honey to make this happen.)

Next, stuff both halves of the passion fruit with your mixture. It doesn't matter if any of the mixture is left over. Place both halves of the fruit together to make a whole fruit once again, and to keep it together tie the red ribbon around the passion fruit.

Place the passion fruit in front of the candle and visualize the passion you wish to reclaim. See this passion right before your mind's eye. Keep the candle burning until right to the end. Now, take the passion fruit and place it in your bedroom, under the bed if possible. When you do this, stale passions will become a thing of the past.

You can do this spell on a Friday at any time of day or night.

You don't listen to me

Sometimes you probably feel that your partner is just not listening to you, that the things you say go in one ear and out the other. This lack of communication can cause frustrations, disappointment, and needless arguments.

You will need:
- 1 small bunch of fresh rosemary leaves
- 5 lemon seeds
- 2 cooking cloves
- 4 coffee beans
- 1 yellow candle
- A small piece of paper that you can write on

On a full-moon night, crush together with a mortar and pestle the lemon seeds, cloves, and coffee beans. Once you've done this, write on the small piece of paper your partner's name and the wish you have that he or she will listen to you more closely.

Next, embed the yellow candle with the aromatic mixture you've created; as you do this, visualize your wish to be listened to. Place the piece of paper under the candle, light the candle, and let it burn all through in a place safe from the wind.

Modification spell

If you wish that your partner was just a little bit more accommodating to your needs, you can achieve your desire with this modification spell.

- 1 letter-size (or A4-size) piece of red paper
- 1 blue pen
- 1 red ribbon

The modification you desire can be as detailed as you want it to be, but make sure there's only one thing you wish to modify. Don't confuse the universe with lots of different modifications. This is not a binding spell. A modification simply means modifying a person's behavior without karmic retaliation. Make sure you are honest with your modification, and that you don't try to control the situation or the issue.

The modification could be as easy as "I modify you to be a little tidier around the house" or "I modify you to be more caring toward me," but you can never modify your partner unnecessarily or for domination. Remember that these are white spells, and white spells need to stay white. Modifications are kinder when you don't do a complicated ritual.

On the piece of paper write:

> I, [your name], *modify you*, [your partner's name], *to* [modification desired].

Once you've written out your modification, roll the paper into a small tube and wrap it with the red ribbon to keep it in place. Carry this roll with you at all times, and whenever you touch it, the modification will work to your advantage.

Hard times

Tension and disharmony in the home can come about due to rough times or difficult financial situations. This tension can bring terrible stress to any relationship, so that even the littlest things start to make you both miserable and bring nothing but hard times and altercations into your home.

You will need:

- 2 white candles
- 1 sewing pin
- 1 charcoal tablet
- ½ teaspoon of dry rosemary leaves
- ½ teaspoon of lavender
- 2 frankincense small nuggets (similar to those used in churches)
- A photograph of you and your partner during happier times
- Matches or a lighter
- A glass bowl

With the pin, carve your name on one candle and your partner's name on the other. While holding and concentrating on the candle with your name, visualize the hard times you're going through and focus on the inner peace you wish for. Do the same thing with the candle bearing your partner's name, and then light them both.

Now, look at the photo of both of you. As you do so, remember what life was like before your current problems, when the love and bond you both shared was stronger, and wish away the hard times you're currently going through.

Fill up the bowl with sand or dirt from outside. Doing so will protect the glass from breaking once you light the tablet, and it will protect you from getting burned. While you're outside, place the charcoal tablet on top of the dirt or sand in the bowl. Light the tablet until it starts sizzling.

Now, put the rosemary, frankincense, and lavender on top of the charcoal tablet and smell the unmistakable aroma that will bring peace and harmony and will get you both through these difficult times. Bring this bowl all over your home in order to cleanse your home of all negativity.

Once you've finished, place the bowl in front of the photograph and the candles, and let the charcoal tablet sizzle out. Allow the candles to burn all the way to the end for peace and harmony. By the time you've finished this spell, you'll already be feeling the peace within you, your partner, and your home.

Your friends don't come first

If your partner spends more time with friends than with you, you need to do this spell to bring your partner back home and back to you.

You will need:
- 1 candle, the color of your partner's star sign
- 1 sewing pin
- 1 photograph of you
- 1 pair of your partner's shoes

Write your partner's name on the candle with the pin. Light the candle while thinking of your partner coming home to you and not out with friends. As you do so, say:

"Home is where I am and home is where you should be."

Now take the photo of yourself and place it inside your partner's shoes, and home your partner will come to spend more time with you.

Keep the shoes in front of the candle until it burns down, and keep the photo inside the shoes for one full week. Do this spell again every other week for a month, or as often as is necessary.

Busy at work, no time for love

Nobody likes it when their partner works late every night to please the boss. When your partner works too hard, it can put a strain on your relationship, your sex life, and your special family time.

You will need:

- 1 blue candle
- 1 red drawstring bag
- 3 tonka beans
- 3 pecans
- ½ teaspoon of poppy seeds

When your partner is working late, light the blue candle and concentrate on why your partner is working at such an hour. Place the tonka beans, the pecans, and the poppy seeds in the drawstring bag. Tie the drawstring bag tightly so nothing can fall out.

Place the drawstring bag over the candle and let the flames heat the seeds, the beans, and the nuts. As you do this, go clockwise over the flame as many times as you wish and say in a strong voice:

"A hard day's work you have done
and for right now it's enough.
Come home and relax and be with the ones you love."

Place the little red drawstring bag in front of the candle and let it stay there until the candle burns out. Then place the drawstring bag under your partner's pillow where it won't be found. Late nights at work will soon be a thing of the past.

Do you love me?

It's difficult to have feelings for someone but not know where you stand, because the other person isn't in touch with his or her own feelings.

You will need:
- 1 pink candle
- 1 teaspoon of lavender buds

- 1 teaspoon of marjoram
- 2 cherries attached by the same stem
- 1 white shallow plate

Hold the pink candle in your hands and visualize the person you love. Search deep within the other person and bring out the feelings they have for you. Say:

> *"Search your heart and tell me true the*
> *feelings you hold deep within your soul."*

Now light the candle and stand it on the white plate; make sure the candle stays in place by putting a little wax on the plate. Make a circle with the lavender buds and the marjoram around the candle on the plate. As you do this, have in mind the truth you want to hear, be it love or friendship.

Gently hold the two cherries in your hands and place the cherries around the candle without tearing them apart.

This spell can be done whenever you wish, and as many times as you wish, but for maximum strength do it on a full-moon night. Let the candle burn through to the end. Scatter the marjoram and the lavender buds to the wind, and bury the cherries under a flower-flourishing bush.

The truth and nothing but the truth

The only way a relationship can survive is by being honest and truthful with your partner no matter how bad things are. Remember, you can live with the truth but you can't live a lie.

You will need:

- 1 red candle
- 1 handful of peppercorns
- 1 teaspoon of orange rinds

Light the red candle and visualize the person you think is lying to you. Say:

> *"No more lies will you ever say to me.*
> *Speak the truth and nothing more."*

Rub the peppercorns and the orange rinds in your hands and let them fall gently on top of the candle's flame. As you do this, say:

"Lies be gone; be true to your soul and our love."

Let the candle burn to the end. Put the remaining peppercorns and orange rinds where your partner will never find them.

Let me go

If you no longer love your partner for whatever reason, he or she will usually feel betrayed and won't be able to let go as quickly as you have. This sense of betrayal can make the situation difficult for both of you—and can lead to anger, persecution, or even violence from your now ex-partner. Or it could even consume your partner and cause an emotional breakdown.

Don't be angry with your ex, who is going through a letting-go period. Just be patient and remember that you once loved this person. Be as tolerant as you can. By doing this simple spell, you can help your ex through the process of grieving and letting go.

You will need:

- 1 pink candle

- 1 candle in the color of your ex's star sign
- 1 candle in the color of your own star sign
- ½ meter (just over 1½ feet) of pink ribbon

Light the pink candle and send your ex peace of mind and the knowledge that everything is going to be all right. After you've done this, tie together with the pink ribbon both of the candles in your star sign colors and say:

"Once we were tight together like these two candles, but we can no longer be; there is no love for you within me."

Now, with both of your hands, break both candles in half at the same time. The breaking of the candles represents the breakup of your relationship; your ex will finally understand it is futile to continue pursuing you—and will instead get on with his or her life.

six

Negative Love Magic

Once we find romantic love, we don't want anyone to stand in its way or, even worse, to take it away from us. Unfortunately, some people out there use negative magic to steal away the romantic love of others—but you must never let that happen to you!

Those who would use negative love magic against you do so in order to destroy your happiness at all costs. They are obsessive and single-minded in this quest, and they don't care who gets hurt as long as they can get what they want—your romantic partner. When they're obsessed with a particular individual, those who practice negative magic have no scruples or morals and will stop at nothing to obtain their goal.

You can usually tell if your partner has been love-cursed by his or her actions. The first clue comes when your partner starts acting in unusual ways and exhibiting erratic behavior from one day to the next. If you observe this sort of behavior, you'll automatically feel it—but don't confuse negative magical workings with manipulation.

In other words, you need to be certain someone else is really using negative forces against your partner—and that the problem isn't you wanting to keep your partner even after he or she has fallen out of love with you. Make sure you use magic without manipulation. If your partner doesn't love you anymore, then let them go. Remember that to love someone also means letting that person go when he or she no longer wants to stay with you. Why use magic to keep someone who doesn't love you? The only reason someone under such a spell would stay with you is because you've manipulated love.

In order to be certain your partner or loved one is under a spell, and to ensure you're using magic for the right reasons, you must ask yourself the following questions:

- Is there someone in your life at this time who has shown an interest in your partner?
- If there is, has this person been overly friendly and given your partner any gifts?
- Has this person wanted to be alone with your partner and tried to exclude you from any plans the two of them have made together?
- Is this person interested in magic?
- Does this person avoid looking you in the eyes?
- Does your partner talk extensively about this person?
- Has your partner told you that he or she wants a new adventure and is willing to leave your relationship to get it, but isn't sure why?
- Does your partner have an ashen look on his or her face?
- Has you partner lost any personal effects, such as socks, shoes, pants, combs, brushes, or even undergarments? Have these items gone missing without any reasonable explanation?

If you can answer yes to 75 percent or more of these questions, you have a problem that needs to be dealt with as soon as possible. Protecting love is one of the most courageous things you will ever do.

Stop in the name of love

If someone is using dark-love workings to take away the person you love, this spell is one you have to do.

You will need:

- 1 large piece of paper
- 1 teaspoon of witch hazel
- 1 teaspoon of raw brown sugar
- 1 red ribbon

Write the name of your loved one on the large piece of paper. Place the witch hazel and the brown sugar on top of the name and wrap it all up in the paper. Tie the little package with the red ribbon and place it under the bed of the one you love. Doing all this will make it difficult for anyone else to take away what is yours. This spell will keep your loved one safe in your home and in your bed!

Not my partner

Just as you would purchase theft insurance for your home and its contents, so too should you do this spell to keep a person with negative thoughts and intentions from stealing your loved one.

You will need:

- 1 Adam and Eve root
- 1 pink candle
- 1 rose incense stick
- 1 red drawstring bag
- 1 carnelian crystal

Burn the rose incense stick and light the pink candle. While you're doing that, visualize your partner or spouse and think about how deeply in love with each other you are. Now, visualize the person trying to take your partner away from you; in your mind, place an imaginary stamp on this person's forehead and mail her or him all the way to Japan, staying far away from the one you love.

Next, hold the Adam and Eve root and the carnelian crystal in your hand. Run both of these over the smoke from the incense and candle, thinking only about the one you love staying home. Place both the crystal and the root in your little red drawstring bag. Put the bag under your partner's pillow, and the one trying to steal away your love will soon be packing up and going away.

Take your eyes away from my lover

Sometimes one particular person wants what is yours and will go to any lengths to get it. Don't just stand there and watch this sham take away what you have built and know to be honest and true. Before you do anything, trust your partner. But if you find that the other person is still trying to take away what is yours, you have every right to protect your relationship.

You will need:
- 1 black candle
- 10 peppercorns
- 1 small blue cloth

Light the black candle while you visualize the one who has intentions toward your partner. Embed every one of the ten peppercorns deep within the candle's wax. With each peppercorn you embed, say in a loud voice with strength and courage:

> *"Keep away from my love,* [the name of your partner]*!*
> *You can't have him* [or *her*] *and you never will."*

Once you've finished, snuff out the candle and wrap it up in the blue cloth. Doing so will cool the other's passion for the one you love. Place the cloth and candle inside your freezer and keep them there until the issue is resolved in your favor.

Peace

Negative energies need discord and arguments in order to feed, and they will never be able to penetrate your home as long as there is peace within it.

You will need:

- 1 white candle
- 5 cooking cloves
- 1 teaspoon of rosemary leaves
- 1 charcoal tablet
- 1 bowl filled with sand

On a moonless Saturday night, light the white candle while thinking only about the peace and protection you want in your home. Then go outside and light the charcoal tablet on top of the sand in the bowl. Bring the bowl back inside when the initial smoke has dispersed and a red charcoal tablet has been left on top of the sand.

Now add three of the cloves and sprinkle half of the rosemary on top of the charcoal tablet. By now, you'll be able to see and smell the aromatic smoke, and sense the protection it provides.

Carry this bowl around your residence in a clockwise direction; you are spreading protective and peaceful energies all around your home. When the smoke begins to die down, put the remaining cloves and the leftover rosemary on top of the charcoal tablet.

Repeat this spell every Saturday and Tuesday for as long as you need to protect the peace in your home from those who would take it away.

Get rid of bad luck from the past
Get rid of the wrongs imposed by another, as these are harmful to your relationship.

You will need:
- 1 sewing pin
- 1 teaspoon of olive oil
- 1 black candle
- 1 green candle

You must first recall when the bad luck started in your relationship. When you have an approximate date in mind, place a few drops of olive oil in your hands and rub them on the black candle from the center up and then from the center down.

Take the pin and etch on the black candle the date the bad luck began, followed by a dash and the date on which you are performing the spell. On the green candle, write the current date with the same pin, followed again by a dash. This time, after the dash, write the year 2199.

Light the black candle and visualize it burning to the end and melting all the bad luck in your relationship.

Then light the green candle as you visualize your relationship as it once was—full of life, love, and luck.

Let both candles consume all the way to the end. You can do this spell on a full moon and at any time on a Saturday.

seven

Relationships and Love Healing

*L*ove is beautiful, but at the same time it can be emotionally exhausting. Some take for granted love that is so freely given. Others abuse the love they receive without respect or consequences. Then there are those who never say no to love even if they are in an abusive relationship. But there are also people who are quick to let love go without fighting for it because they lack the energy to keep working on the relationship.

Most people in an abusive relationship (even one that is verbally and not physically abusive), or a relationship with an alcoholic, must let love go for their own good and for their own peace of mind if their partner is not willing to seek outside help to save the relationship. Yet if both people even in these types of relationships are willing to work at it and seek counseling, then there still may be a chance to save the relationship. But if your partner isn't willing to take that extra step, then you'll need to accept that you must let go of love for your own good.

A dear friend of mine fell in love with a drug addict. He actually told her he was an addict during the first couple of weeks they were dating. My friend believed that he would give up drugs for her since he loved her. Well, this man did try to quit drugs and took all the necessary steps to start his rehabilitation, but he just wasn't ready. Every time my friend found out that he had lied to her and was taking drugs behind her back, it cost her pain and much anguish.

Here they were, these two people deeply in love with each other, but my friend knew she could not help her boyfriend at that point, and so she finally walked away from him. They kept in touch, but they both realized it was impossible to even try a relationship while he was still abusing drugs.

I always used to tell my friend that if it's not meant to be in this lifetime, it will be in the next. The good news is that this man has since then truly given up drugs, has been drug-free for years now, and he and my friend are now living happily ever after.

Sometimes we have to walk away from these types of relationships for our own mental stability. My friend is one of many people in such a situation who did the right thing; she walked away from her boyfriend to let him deal with his own demons. If a relationship is meant to be, it will be—no matter what steps you take to get there. And if it's not meant to be, then the universe has a better plan for your romantic love. This goes for all types of difficult relationships. It's hard to walk away from them because the love you feel for the other person pulls you to a point at which you can't see the wrongs that are affecting you. For this reason, people say love is blind—and it *is* blind. Everyone around you can see the problem, but you are blind to it because you are in love.

The cluster of spells in this chapter will help you to stay strong and get through the trying times in a difficult relationship; I assure you there will be a spell here that's relevant to your situation. Always seek out a true friend when you are troubled or lost, or go to a counselor for professional help and advice. Remember that no matter how difficult the relationship is, there is always a way out if you want it. *You* are in control of your life. Search your heart and don't let others pull you down to their level. You are special and deserve the best in life and love. Never forget that.

Heal the love within

All relationships are governed by emotions. Once we've been hurt by the one we love, we can spend weeks or even months trying to get over that emotion and the resentment we feel toward our partner. Whether the situation is your fault or theirs, there is healing to be done.

You will need:

- 1 pink candle
- ½ cup of pineapple juice
- 1 teaspoon of blue food dye
- The petals of a white flower
- 1 dash of rose or lavender water
- 1 teaspoon of rock salt

Prepare a warm bath, preferably on a Friday. When you're ready to begin the spell, light the pink candle and visualize the wrongs done to you burning away to nothing.

Slowly add the rest of the ingredients to the bathwater. Let the water absorb everything you are putting in it while you visualize peace, happiness, and forgiveness in your heart. Once you've done this, submerge yourself in the healing water and feel its essence traveling to the center of your soul and washing away all your hurts.

Stay in the bath for as long as you like. When you're ready to come out, pat yourself dry, which will seal the healing energy within you. Don't shower or rinse again for a full twenty-four hours.

Understanding and forgiving infidelity

Infidelity is one of the hardest things a relationship will ever have to face, but romantic love can sometimes survive it— even though the pain of the betrayal may not diminish and your sense of trust may not return to what it was before.

The first thing you need to ask yourself after discovering infidelity is whether or not you want to work to forgive this betrayal. If you do, then ask your partner if he or she is also willing to put the infidelity behind you both and work with you on mending the wrongs done. If your partner is willing to take this path, then you must resolve to work to forgive, understand, and move on without bringing up the infidelity at every turn.

You will need:

- 1 teaspoon of nutmeg
- 1 teaspoon of angelica
- 1 teaspoon of palm oil
- A mortar and pestle
- 1 blue candle
- 1 candle in the color of the star sign of the person who was unfaithful to you (see page 5)
- 1 sewing pin
- 1 photo of you both together in happier times
- Pink and blue ribbon (from your Love Box, if you're keeping one)

On a Sunday morning when the sun is out, mix together the nutmeg, angelica, and palm oil with the mortar and pestle.

Add more palm oil if you need it to make a thick paste. On the blue candle, etch your name with the pin. Next, anoint the candle with some of the healing, loving paste you've just mixed together. As you do so, visualize yourself forgiving the pain and suffering caused by the infidelity. Also visualize your heart's willingness to forgive and move on.

Now pick up your partner's star-sign candle. Use the pin to write your partner's name on that candle as you visualize him or her fully devoted to working on your relationship and never hurting you in this way ever again. Anoint this candle with the healing paste you've mixed, but this time only add the paste to the bottom half of the candle, the half farthest away from the wick end. As you do this, visualize your partner never straying again.

Hold the photo of you both in your hands and then place it over your heart, visualizing happy times once again. Anoint the photo with the rest of the paste. Once you've done all this, roll up the picture. To keep the photo rolled up, wrap the pink and blue ribbons around it with six knots. Place the rolled-up photo in front of the candles.

Light the candles and visualize the hurt and suffering subsiding, allowing you to understand and move on. Let both candles burn through right to the end. Once they've burned through, take the photo and put it under your mattress on your partner's side of the bed. Don't remove it from there until you're comfortable that the necessary healing has occurred.

Seek aid from an addictive relationship

There are different types of addictive or dysfunctional relationships, but they all have one thing in common: they hurt whoever is in them. You must be the one to break away from the never-ending cycle of dysfunction, whether it is a cycle of verbal or physical abuse, out-of-control jealousy, or something else such as alcoholism or drug addiction.

If you are in this type of relationship, you need to ask yourself: Do I need this? Am I strong enough to handle this relationship? Do I want to stay in this relationship even though I know there isn't much light at the end of the tunnel? You must be honest with yourself and remember that every dysfunction and addiction comes from a refusal to face a possibly painful past.

Face the facts: if your partner refuses to seek help, then he or she is preferring to drown in self-pity. If you think you can help such a person even after a refusal of professional counseling, you are wrong. Your partner must acknowledge that there's a problem that's damaging the relationship before you'll be able to help him or her. Even if there may be hope for both of you down the road, you don't need to watch your partner destroy his or her life or your own. Sometimes you really must leave the one you love for the good of both of you. This spell will help you to get in touch with the inner you as you seek support and direction from your guides.

You will need:

- 1 white candle
- 1 glass of fresh water
- 1 white flower

At a time when you're home alone and no one could possibly disturb you, gently drop the petals of the white flower into the glass of clear, fresh water. Place the white candle next to the glass of water. Now, light the candle and watch the candle's flame burn.

Think of your guardian or your angel, whichever one you believe is always by your side, and seek his or her help. Say out loud:

"I seek the wisdom of those who care for me
to help me find the answers to my addictive love.
If I should stay or go is the wisdom I seek within you and me.
Help me find the answers and let me be true to my heart and
the ones I love with all my might.
I seek peace to move on, or strength if I should not.
Let me uncover the answer I seek,
so as not to be addicted to an unhealthy relationship."

Once you're finished speaking, reflect on what you've said and listen deep within your soul. Your answers will come as the days pass by.

Let the white candle burn right to the end and place the glass of water with the white flower petals in a high place, so that no one can touch it before the answers you are seeking arrive.

~ closing ~

When you find love, keep it. But if you lose it, it will find you again. Hold on to your soul mate. If you don't find your soul mate in this lifetime, you certainly will in the next. Never lose hope, as love is nearby. Be true to your heart, and don't stay where your love is no longer needed. Remember, there is another love waiting around the corner who will hold you and keep you breathless forevermore in this lifetime and the next.

Blessed be,
Ileana

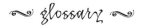

Glossary

Abyss

A dark place that unconsciously feeds our depression or negative state of mind.

Affirmation

A positive statement one makes about oneself or a situation.

Aura field

The field that surrounds all of us, the colors that radiate outside our physical bodies.

Dark love

Manipulating love for one's own selfish needs.

Broken heart

The intense feeling of loss after the end of a relationship.

Chakras

The seven light points of our bodies.

Charcoal tablets

Carbon used to burn incense.

Crystals

Semiprecious stones used to promote health, happiness, luck, and spirituality if carried or used with intent.

Essential oils

Oils extracted from flowers, plants, or resins.

Etheric field

The field of pure energy that radiates outside our physical bodies.

Human nature

Behavior of people resulting from their culture, attitudes, or values.

Karma

The law of the universe: "what goes around, comes around."

The Love Box

A box in which we keep all that we need to conduct a love spell.

Magic

The use of natural energies and positive visualization to create change in our lives.

Magical supplier/New Age store

A shop that sells ingredients and equipment necessary for magical spells.

Manipulative love

Forcing the love of another when it doesn't exist.

Positive visualization

Remaining positive while visualizing your needs to both the universe and yourself.

Romantic love

The love we share when we are in a romantic relationship

Self-love

The love you feel for yourself when you accept who you are.

The "tools"

Items and ingredients necessary for conducting spells.

index